in 1947. He studied at Vermont and at the Neighborhood Playhouse School of Theater in New York. He has taught at Goddard College, the Yale School of Drama and New York University, and lectures at the Atlantic Theater Company, of which he is a founding member. He is the author of the plays *The Cryptogram, Oleanna, Speed-the-Plow, Glengarry Glen Ross, American Buffalo* and *Sexual Perversity in Chicago*. His films include, as screenwriter, *The Postman Always Rings Twice, The Verdict, The Untouchables, The Edge, Wag the Dog* and *The Life of David Gale*, and as writer/director, *House of Games, Homicide, Things Change, The Spanish Prisoner* and *State and Main*. He is also the author of children's books, four books of essays, two novels, and two books on drama, *True and False* and *Three Uses of the Knife*. His plays have won the Pulitzer Prize and the Obie Award.

**also as a Methuen Student Edition,
with comprehensive notes and commentary*

David Mamet

Dr Faustus

Methuen Drama

Published by Methuen 2005

1 3 5 7 9 10 8 6 4 2

First published in the United Kingdom
in 2005 by Methuen Publishing Limited
11–12 Buckingham Gate
London SW1E 6LB

Methuen Publishing Limited Reg. No. 3543167

A CIP catalogue record for this book is available from
the British Library

ISBN 0 413 77408 2

Typeset by Country Setting, Kingsdown, Kent
Printed and bound in Great Britain by
Bookmarque Ltd, Croydon, Surrey

Caution

Dr Faustus

The world premiere of *Dr Faustus* was presented at the
Magic Theatre, San Francisco, on 28 February 2004.
The cast was as follows:

Faustus	David Rasche
Wife	Sandra Lindquist
Friend	Colin Stinton
Magus	Dominic Hoffman
Boy	Benjaman Beecroft/Nathan Wexler

Director	David Mamet
Set Designer	Peter Larkin
Lighting Designer	Russell H. Champa
Costume Designer	Fumiko Bielefedt
Assistant Director	Emily Halpern
Magic Consultants	Deceptive Practices; Ricky Jay and Michael Weber

Characters

Faustus
His **Wife**
His **Friend**, *Fabian*
Magus
Boy, *Faustus's son*

Setting

Act One: Faustus's home, on the occasion of a party for his son

Act Two: variously, Earth, Heaven and Hell

Act One

At rise, we see the portico of **Faustus***'s home. Large double doors open on to a room hung with tinsel and streamers, a party scene gotten up as a fantasy.*

Faustus*'s* **Wife** *is involved in decoration.* **Faustus** *enters and looks around. Pause. He holds a sheet of paper in his hand.*

Faustus   It seems a very dream.

Wife   It is a dream. Delightful, as it is temporary.

Faustus   Temporary.

Wife   How otherwise?

Faustus   To what do you refer?

Wife   Have I mistook you?

Faustus   What is it you indict of transience?

Wife   Of transience – the decor.

Faustus   The decor, of course.

Wife   Which, you remark, will serve but the day's brief turn . . .

Faustus   Of course . . .

Wife   . . . divert the child, and then . . .

Faustus   How is the boy?

Wife   He would be thrilled to find you at this unaccustomed hour. What has released you . . . ?

Faustus   And where is Fabian . . . ?

Wife   I believe he marshals the festivities. I beg your pardon, are you anxious for his news?

Faustus   What news?

Wife   Today is Friday . . .

Faustus Yes . . .

Wife He generally brings the gazette. Are you cold,
Faustus? The day is cold.

Faustus The chill livens the mind. Life grows in the cold.
Does it not?

Wife It grows however you should bid.

Faustus My bidding cannot alter its growth.

Wife But it shall affect how I perceive it.

Faustus I believe I have completed my work. (*Of the paper
in his hand.*)

Wife What . . . ?

Faustus I believe I have completed it.

Wife Your most sanguine of expectations could not put the
end sooner than years.

Faustus So indeed I thought.

Wife Then how . . . ?

Faustus It rests in the rendition of the false. Which, like
a bridal veil, could not be lifted by force − solely through
devotion. (*He hands her the paper.*)

Wife I cannot follow it. The argument's beyond me.

Faustus Then take me on faith, and pardon me.

Wife For what conceivable sin?

Faustus To leach attention from another's feast. How is
the child?

Wife He loves you. You repeat yourself.

Faustus Then you may claim a forfeit.

Wife Your soul.

Faustus Have I not given it?

Wife How can you live without your soul?

Faustus It flourishes without me. While within it was bound by my vice, and vanity, each step for its supposed cultivation only brought it blight. Since consecrated, I observe it to grow strong. Its reproofs are of the most gentle, and its instructions delight.

Wife What has it taught you?

Faustus To yield, to wait, to hope, to believe. In fine, it has taught gratitude.

Wife Smile, then, on your faults, as those do who love you. For all must wax and wane.

Faustus Indeed?

Wife Must I quote you the Moon?

Faustus Oh, simple and good soul, are you not my salvation?

Wife As you are mine.

Faustus Who counted himself honoured merely to be your support.

Wife Do we not profit, nay, thrive, nay, delight in your wisdom?

Faustus It is derivative.

Wife Must not all wisdom be?

Faustus Must it?

Wife As it derives from God. Our excellence is not in Creation, which is the Lord's, but in our humble wonderment.

Faustus Which you indict me of?

Wife I do.

Faustus You honour me.

Wife I must see to the boy.

Faustus   Stay.

Wife   He is somewhat overborne by the excitement.

Faustus   Stay. This one moment. Anchor me.

Wife   This may suffice. (*Hands him a sheet of paper.*)

Faustus   What is it?

Wife   His gift to you.

Faustus   'Tis his day for gifts.

Wife   Does he not long to pace you in all things? Who are his god? You fret, he frets; you work, he mimics you; you prepare a gift, so must he . . . and his mind, formed like yours, revolves ever on the one planetary theme.

Faustus   Whose name is?

Wife   He pines for you.

Faustus   You give him to understand . . . my work . . .

Wife   Which names his enemy, but cannot diminish his longing.

Faustus   My sweet son.

Wife   We have all fretted.

Faustus   Fretted for me?

Wife   *With* you, say, rather – *with* you – in your seclusion.

Faustus   Yes, I know.

Wife   Now know the extent. His poem to you. (*She gestures at her sheet of paper.*)

Faustus (*reads*)
   'Heavy, heavy the hired man
   Weary, how weary the willing hand.
   One for the heart, one for the head
   One for the lad who tarries abed . . .'

He stays abed . . . ?

Wife   . . .'tis but the figure.

Faustus (*reads*)
  'Three swift swallows in the summer sky . . .
  Gone in the Twinkling of an eye.
  What mystic light, illumes the night
  A father's care . . .'

Pause.

This is the son's love. Full-grown man cannot compass it.
But in nostalgia for the infant state . . . that hopeless love of
the omnipotent. Sad, savage longing.

Wife   Sad?

Faustus   Is it not?

Wife   It turns joyful. Read to the end . . .

Faustus   I recollect, now, for the one half-instant − that
brief, child mind, when all good dwelt in self-consuming
worship. How might a man deserve it?

Wife   One may but treasure it. Come to him.

Faustus   In the one moment. My hand to my heart −

Wife   Then I must go.

Faustus   Again, is he unwell?

Wife   But overtaxed, anxious for the celebration.

Faustus   Go then, be thou my emissary. Relate my delight
at his composition, and offer th' appropriate salutations, as
fitting one scribe to his brother upon this festive, so on . . .
Bid him allow me to compose myself, after my labor, and I
come to him complete.

Wife   Complete, and abandoned to the festivities.

Faustus   Like a newly convinced addict.

Wife   And our profound congratulations on the completion
of your work. I lack the words . . . might you take them for
said?

Faustus   And put so prettily.

Wife   Where?

Faustus   In your visage – see to the child.

She exits. **Faustus** *looks at the paper.*

Faustus   'One for the heart, one for the head / One for
the lad who tarries abed . . .' Poor child. His work now
complete, he, like his father, is cursed to begin again. For, as
much as the work partakes of divine afflatus, to that same
extreme one must again tempt, cajole, entreat, and
importune the gods. The artist weathercock now ratifying
north, now northwest, and we serially nod delight at each
fresh revelation. Hush, he is working; hush, he is done. See:
our poor petted Sisyphus, watch his labor now devolve from
him. Both fame and failure apportioning but self-revulsion.
The mind is a mill which can incessant turn, till its mere
operation focus the stress inward and the stones grind
themselves to dust.

Enter the **Friend**.

Friend   This is a curious greeting for an anniversary.

Faustus   Fabian.

Friend   How is the boy?

Faustus   I was to go to him – I have forgotten. Lord, hear
my plea. My sin is great, pardon my self-absorption.

Friend   So may we indict any man.

Faustus   And myself the chief malefactor.

Friend   Why?

Faustus   The greater the gift the greater the shame in
malfeasance, e'en here I sin in pride, how can you stomach
me?

Friend   Doth not contrition mitigate your pride?

Faustus   It is a counterfeit. Like the rich, I trust to the soft brush of rhetoric, to rasp from me the stench of crime.

Friend   Shall nothing cleanse you?

Faustus   Mine is the Sin of the Confessional. Of one whose depth of contrition, howe'er impersonated, nay, howe'er felt, may never plumb the depth of his duplicity. I am a fraud. Whose prayer is not thanks, but anxiety: let me be played off, e'er I am discovered.

Friend   Not today, not today, good Master, which is a feast day, when we are bid to drink, to rest, to celebrate.

Faustus   What of philosophy?

Friend   And let philosophy succor itself, in whate'er it may consist.

Faustus   While we?

Friend   Grope blindly, as Your Honor knows, in hope of that good morsel, heady liquor, or compliant wench.

Faustus   Do we then, like the beasts, live solely for repletion?

Friend   On the which note might I dare importune you for refreshment?

Faustus   Do I construe you to mean, you find philosophy less than a noble task?

Friend   I've seen, these many years, that you enjoy when, at close of day, you have matched this word to that emotion.

Faustus   You find it an unworthy pastime?

Friend   Who am I to balk another of his freak? I knew a villain, said he lived to count the stars. Each darkness found him, with his pen and ledger, out of the house, happy as a grig.

Faustus   . . . It pleased him.

Friend   He called it his life's work.

Faustus   To number the stars.

Friend   So he said. Until that day he wandered out of bounds into a neighbor's copse, and was killed by the gamekeeper.

Faustus   The gamekeeper mistook the fellow's errand.

Friend   Oh no, he reckoned it aright.

Faustus   How so?

Friend   Each night, my friend took up his ledger and trod out, it was in fact to lie with the gamekeeper's wife.

Faustus   Aha.

Friend   *And* daughter.

Faustus   I see your man was a prodigy.

Friend   Sir, you don't know the half of it.

Faustus   Which distinguishes me from the gamekeeper's wife.

Friend   . . . *and* daughter . . .

Faustus   . . . as you said.

Friend   *and* son, for all we know.

Faustus   So much is hidden from us . . . (*Pause.*) You balk me of my prerogative melancholy.

Friend   You have enrolled me as your foil. Permit me my turn. Again, might you supply a drink, to a traveler, come from the cold unfeeling world?

Faustus   Ah, have you brought the journal?

Friend   The journal, no.

Faustus   You have not?

Friend   But is it Friday?

Faustus   Returned, with its noted regularity.

Friend   I do not have the journal, no.

Faustus   Oh, my friend, you are damned to Hell. Heaven must shun you, as you use its gifts so ill.

Friend   What gift?

Faustus   Mendacity. Give me the gazette.

Friend   I do not have it.

Faustus   Give it in any case.

Friend   I would not vex you on this party day.

Faustus   I warrant you I shall survive what your reluctance indicates as their displeasure.

Friend   They have, we must note, historically praised you.

Faustus   They praise me, as they praise the mother of the bride, to mask their own concupiscence. What is their praise, they are, as dolt schoolchildren bent over their sums, they round their inclusivities into the most proximate low error. Their censure and applause are one. But th' extorted approbation of the mob. Crowds who cry up this slaughterer, that thief as great? Give me sufficient ink and paper, I'll make a dog's bone beloved of the world.

Friend   Do you shun fame?

Faustus   I accept it. I pursue knowledge.

Friend   Would you then publish your work anonymously?

Faustus   Discovered, I confess. Am I a libertine? A thief? A murderer? I covet fame. And, like the criminal, I plead first, what have I done, and next, who suffered? Yes. I would have fame. For my works, and fame surpassing them, till Faustus's renown shines free of accomplishment. Read me the journal.

Friend   Read it to you?

Faustus   The honest man – must in good modesty avert his gaze. It is a disgraceful proclivity. The journals.

Friend   To write them?

Faustus   To *read* them. To write them is a crime against nature. What do they say of me?

Friend   Pray, delay it past this festive time. How is the boy?

Faustus   He has a cold upon the chest. Read the report to me.

Friend (*takes out a newspaper and reads*)   That . . .

Faustus   Please . . .

Friend   . . . my eyes as you know are weak.

Faustus   Supply the lack with concentration.

Friend   'Our celebrated polymath, our local champion . . .'

Faustus   Now we enlarge the epigram: even a dead pig finds a truffle. Read on . . .

Friend   'Faustus, our premier: physician, philosopher, savant-scientist . . .'

Faustus   A linguistic supererogation . . .

Friend   '. . . having labored for,' etcetera . . .

Faustus   I shall respond to them.

Friend   '. . . proceeds, our sources inform us . . .'

Faustus   Who might these sources be?

Friend   Friends of yourself, and friends of knowledge?

Faustus   Ah yes, the hopeful constituency of the seekers-after-light, the talented who worship genius, the mediocre, who doubt its existence. Whom do I lack?

Friend   The average man. You omit that creature.

Faustus   Has he, then, heard of me?

Friend   Does he not read the journal?

Faustus   As the mariner rivets his gaze to the lighthouse.

Friend   What must he make of you – Faustus?

Faustus   Please . . . ?

Friend   In truth, accomplished, celebrated, wealthy, loved . . . how may he compass it? This average man?

Faustus   How can we know? Our Biblia Sacra treats not of him, but of ourself. Say on . . .

Friend   Are you immune?

Faustus   Let's make the trial.

Pause.

Friend   'That we have tired of the oft-reiterated phrase that we may expect, momentarily, the completion of the long awaited . . . ' I had rather not continue.

Faustus   Does it turn combative? (*Pause.*) Does it suggest I have been o'erpraised? And that a new, unsentimental day, judge between merit and nostalgia? Does it suggest 'brief comet, in the firmament, and long-deferred hope of its return . . . '?

Friend   Are you, then, clairvoyant, to read the hidden page?

Faustus   They are a newspaper. How may continued praise be news? It may not. Read on, though I could have writ it.

Friend (*reads*)   '. . . as an uncontracted burden, upon our intellectual establishment; the tax of continued praise for this juvenilia, of long-deferred hope for completion of a notional magnum opus. The repeated postponement of which must call to doubt its very existence . . . Our praise of Faustus . . .'

Faustus   I have completed my work.

Friend   Say again.

Faustus   I have completed it.

Friend   When?

Faustus (*passing him the paper*)   Smudge the fresh ink with your finger, and add your mark to the colophon.

Friend   Would it were so . . .

Faustus   You'd wish it?

Friend   You speak from Parnassus, to him the gods delight to ignore. Will you license me, Faustus, to express my deep honor, and my profound sense of occasion?

Faustus   Equally, my friend, who have supported me. For in my doubt I treasured your belief.

Friend   You doubted, Faustus . . . ?

Faustus   How could I but doubt? Who played with this or that prideful manipulation. Till I found not the piece I sought, but an inversion of the paradigm. I have been a fool occupied with toys. I have misused the gifts vouchsafed to me.

Friend   How possibly?

Faustus   Through the very conjectural disclaimers of worth, each calculated or to increase my fame, or to propitiate nemesis. You wish to ruin a man, praise him for his self-known hypocrisies. For gold's ever fresh-minted in delight, but its worth is untied to the form, but part of the earth's primal store. (*Pause.*) In fine, praise God, and let them say this of me: He was rewarded for his brute persistence. Not for an act but for a submission.

Friend   A submission?

Faustus   For is not the answer constantly before us . . . ?

Friend   And your work treats of the answer?

Faustus   As you say.

Friend   And may you capsulate it?

Faustus   Read . . . Read. Here: it is a mathematic formula. That is all. It is a numeric reduction.

Friend (*takes the paper*)   Surely its study requires diligence.

Faustus   Indeed.

Friend   The computation is abstruse, the equation beyond my mathematic skills.

Faustus   Here is the coda . . .

Friend   How shall I grasp it absent the foundation?

Faustus   Attend –

The **Wife** *enters.*

Wife   Fabian.

Friend   My dear, I understand that I am doubly to felicitate you.

Wife   Fabian, welcome. Faustus . . .

Faustus   In the one moment . . . will it hold?

Wife   For the one moment, of course . . .

Friend (*to* **Wife**)   Will you hear my speech? I shall extemporise th' addition . . .

Wife   With thanks, but presently, I must see to the boy. (*She exits.*)

Friend   Is he unwell?

Faustus   Children, like the Mass, act in the responsive state, they quaver to the air, the Moon, a drop in the glass, the helictic motion of the spheres. How could he otherwise than resonate at my discovery? See, now the very humors in the sway of periodic power.

Friend   Of periodic power.

Faustus (*of his manuscript page*)   See, see here. Read.

Friend   It is beyond me.

Faustus   Read the preamble. See. That number. That all
is reducible to periodicity. To cipher, to a formula, expressed
in number; and that number signifies not quantity . . . not
quantity. But a progression.

Pause.

Friend   . . . I am at a loss, my friend.

Faustus   No – stay – I shall parcel it slowly.

Friend   Fit your description to my limits.

Faustus   Consider the boy.

Friend   For which my felicitations.

Faustus   Many thanks. Now see him age.

Friend   Which, may God in His beneficence permit.

Faustus   Amen, with all my heart. Now we admit him as
a youth, surprised, by first love, later by betrothal, marriage,
and conception. Each, to his eye, a personal, nay
idiosyncratic ebullition. Yet, from our remove, inevitable,
universal.

Friend   Thus?

Faustus   And thus predictable. There is a generalized
periodicity . . . which, once revealed's, encountered every-
where. I instance: the recurrence of drought, famine, fire, and,
by extension, those eruptions we, untutored, understand, as
acts of will: war, civic growth, invention and decay . . . Had
one sufficient remove, one could plot the concordance.

Friend   Of?

Faustus   Of acts of nature, and supposed acts of will. In
short, of human movement. (*Pause.*) There is a consonance.
It is a code. It is called periodicity. It is the secret engine of
the world.

Friend   You here profess to comprehend it?

Faustus   Read.

Pause.

Friend   Is it not blasphemy?

Faustus   Blasphemy and prayer are one. Both assert the existence of a superior power. The first, however, with conviction.

Friend   But should one stray too far . . . ?

Faustus   How might one stray too far?

Friend   Permit me, if I may, to counsel respect for the jocular proclivities we know to be the gods. Were it not better to refrain? Do not tempt fate.

Faustus   What is my charge but to tempt fate? Each time I commence and each conclude?

Friend   Until?

Faustus   Until God recoil at the impertinence? (*Pause.*) He bids the farmer find delight in the pristine, the entrepreneur in the ruined, the philosopher in the occluded. As sentries on the battlement, shall we not be drawn to the edge?

Friend   And cautioned to refrain.

Faustus   Yet incited to leap.

Friend   By?

Faustus   An echo of forgotten power, as in the life of birds.

Friend   Do we descend from birds? Say angels.

Faustus   Both, you remark, can fly.

Friend   You frighten me.

Faustus   Is it not my duty? Hand me the journal – I will respond to them.

Friend   Would I were more intelligent, or to dispute or second your conclusions.

Faustus   Each trade must bear its occupation mark. The ploughman's gnarled hands, the blacksmith's seared forearm.

Friend   And the philosopher?

Faustus   A certain melancholy – the dual conviction of futility and prescience. A cook with but two spices, ever attempting to amend with one, his error with the other. (*Pause.*)   Enough. I have transgressed, not the prerogatives of the gods, but the more comprehensible strictures of good manners. Today's the boy's.

Friend   Indeed.

Faustus   He wrote to me.

Friend   He did?

Faustus   A poem.

Faustus *hands the poem to his* **Friend**. *The* **Friend** *reads the poem.*

Friend
  'What mystic light illumes the night.
  A father's care . . .'

This is a sign of grace.

Faustus   Is that a scientific term?

Friend   Never a cynic but concealed acolyte *in potentia*.

Faustus   And what brave man divulged the theory?

Friend   You did.

Faustus   Your learning does you credit. 'A father's care.' Perhaps it is grace.

Friend   What a concession.

Faustus   Yes, why should I be chosen?

Friend   All are chosen.

Faustus   All are chosen? Then what possible meaning has the term?

Friend   We are all subject to God's grace.

Faustus   Bless me, he treads damn near the theological.

Friend   You say you seek a greater power.

Faustus   A greater power than *that*, certainly.

Friend   Than what?

Faustus   Than *religion*.

Friend   There is no greater power.

Faustus   Then why does one find, under its aegis, nay, in its name, more progressed misery, murder, and starvation than exists in an unbeneficed state of nature? Answer me that and go free.

Friend   Many find it a source of strength.

Faustus   The leaf of the camomile, parboiled in water, conduces to calm. And yet I do not worship it.

Friend   You spoke of a greater power –

Faustus   I spoke of *number*.

Friend   Number.

Faustus   Yes. Not religion, which to the scientific mind cannot be quantified.

Friend   Is it, then, worthless?

Faustus   To the scientist.

Friend   Then how comes religion to cleanse?

Faustus   A candle gains in power as we still warring illumination. Were we to flood the room with light, the object of our interest, of our longing, of our worship is forgot. For it is nothing.

Pause.

Friend   It is salvation.

Faustus   Then seek it. As each man seeks himself, in all things. This is the law of life.

Friend   I understand, of course, your enthusiasm.

Faustus   . . . Your mitigating clause?

Friend   I simply suggest reserve of speech.

Faustus   Speech cannot alter the unfolding of the natural order.

Friend   And what of miracle?

Faustus   Instance it –

Friend   Many invoke Salvation.

Faustus   And many believe in war, yet remark that they do not fight.

Friend   But –

Faustus   Say on.

Friend   To impugn. The power of the Church to save . . .

Faustus   Proclaimed by whom but man?

Friend   Christ's word is divine.

Faustus   Proclaimed . . . ?

Friend   By the Council of Nicaea.

Faustus   Who, if I do not err, were men.

Friend   But this is heresy.

Faustus   Greater than theirs? (*Pause.*) Greater than theirs?

Friend   I do believe it.

Faustus   This too is an equation. There are but two paths by which men may thrive: the direct pursuit of power, and the propitiation of its possessors.

Friend   But some do good.

Faustus   Yes?

Friend   Do you grant it?

Faustus   If it amuses you.

Faustus's Wife *enters.*

Wife   Faustus.

Faustus   One moment. (*Pause.*) Do I vex you? Do I confound? All of your adjurations, to recant, are but reminders to speak hypocritically, as all men speak. (*Pause.*) You fear the impending limit of the circumscribed. You cling to: tradition, reason, custom, common sense, an intelligent submission. And I ask: to what?

Friend   Then what is not to be despised?

Wife   Our love for a child, which seeks nothing for itself.

Faustus   Save immortality.

Wife   I was bid announce your arrival. We take you at your word – he waits for you. I do not mean to vex you in your happy completion . . .

Faustus   No, no. The fault is mine. (*She exits.*) Well, then, you see, the poor philosopher, jerked from his native element of disputation, struggles on the bank. I must go.

Friend   But is there no excellence?

Faustus   Yes. I have troubled you.

Friend   Is all but *number*? I understand you to speak hyperbolically . . .

Faustus   I do not.

Friend   But does naught exist, absent your formula?

Faustus   Else, of what worth the equation?

Friend   But, the ineffable: hope, courage . . .

Faustus   Show it to me.

Friend   In the military.

Faustus   They hone the scabbard while the saber rusts. Bravo the generals.

Friend   Say in the private soldier?

Faustus   He fights from rage, fear, or shame – who does not?

Friend   In the devotion of the pedagogue.

Faustus   To drill the young to say five things about seven books.

Friend   Say, in the law, in jurisprudence.

Faustus   Many remark justice is blind; pity those in her sway, shocked to discover she is also deaf.

Friend   Then in the service of the State.

Faustus   In what consists the State? A salubrity of climate or geography, o'erlaid by the posturings of the suborned; unwashed cupidity, license for murder . . . Oh, if I were king.

Friend   Be still, they might elect you.

Faustus   Heaven forfend.

Friend   And e'en a king's power is circumscribed.

Faustus   As whose is not.

Friend   God's, people say.

Faustus   Then how explain human suffering?

Friend   His power is limitless to do. Ours is curtailed to understand.

Faustus   A good, traditional response.

The **Magus** *appears, with a flourish of drums. He carries a valise marked with a devil's head.*

Faustus   Selah. Who have we here? Is it the Devil . . . Sir, are you the Devil?

Magus   His counterfeit, My Lord, upon the earth.

Wife (*drawn by the sound*)   Faustus, who has engaged the entertainer?

Faustus   Right welcome. Are we not told, of periodic riots of inversion, where we find license to resolve our various superfluities? Heathen societies knew it as orgy, we, their ailing, decadent descendants call it holiday. Here is the last pagan survival welcome, sir – what do you bring?

Magus   Signor, we bring a carnival.

Faustus   Bravo.

Wife   I fear the boy unequal to the entertainment.

Faustus   Then I shall bear the shock.

The **Wife** *retires.*

Faustus   Dare we hope that you come to subvert the natural order?

Magus   As you may judge. Vouchsafe the moment for our preparation, and we shall reveal the occult, and set at defiance: time, space, and logic, law, and decorum.

Faustus   Proceed – proceed, sir, are we not yours?

The **Magus** *performs a magical flourish, and then intones:*

Magus
  Ecco
  The carnival
  Wherein, all rights reversed,
  We abjure hypocrisy
  O blessed traveler,
  Who quits his burden as if ne'er to
  Reassume it
  Cast from you care, disport as before th' invention
    of remorse
  The timid call themselves philosophers,
  The bolder libertines,
  Each, however, once subsumed, becomes the acolyte.
  The disparate revealed as one, the whole as mosaic
  As we shatter the oppressive unities till space, matter,
    thought and life itself are called by the one name
  Jubio!

The **Magus** *does a magical trick.*

Faustus   Oh, sir. Need we fear?

Magus   Naught but the mysteries . . .

Faustus *applauds.*

Faustus   All reverence to the lord of misrule. Honor, of course, to the Creator, but to the inverter, ten thousand times more. Poor ignorant folk, here below, we've glimpsed the world the wrong way round, now may we stare, delighted at the back of the tapestry. Or have we gazed, all our lives, at its inversion? (*To* **Magus**.) What do you say?

Magus   I have prayed for a man to understand me.

Faustus   Am I that man?

Magus   From your speech, sir, I'd have took you for one of the confraternity.

Faustus   No, I am but a poor projector. Yours is the core of accomplishment.

Magus   The core, sir?

Faustus   Are we not told, the jesters of a wiser day made all whole in shaking a skull at their masters? Have you heard that tale?

Magus   I have, but cannot credit it.

Faustus   Nor I, for where, among the great, do we find self-depreciation? (*He takes up the gazette.*) Nor should one feel the need, when these exist, detractors by profession – eunuch compilers, swine . . . (*Reads.*) 'Our petted savant . . . fat on the leavings of a prior fame' . . . Another trick, sir, loose me a diverting marvel.

Friend   Shall we not await the child?

Faustus   Do not subvert the flow of the performance. Charm me, from the world.

Magus   I can but conjure, sir, as I am skilled, which extends but to the distraction of the uninformed . . .

Friend   Behold another of your confraternity. (*Of the paper.*)
Continue.

Magus   Bid me.

Faustus (*of the newspaper*)   Make this foul indictment
disappear.

Magus (*takes the newspaper, and, with a flourish, disappears it*)
Ecco. It vanishes.

Faustus   No!

Magus   Sir, to the contrary.

Faustus   Oh, bravo.

Magus   I did not o'erextend my brief . . . ?

Faustus   Indeed you did. Well done and excellently
improvised. My hand.

Magus   Most honored.

Faustus   To have fooled the philosopher.

Magus   One finds, in my profession, sir, the greater the
intellect, the more ease in its misdirection.

Faustus   One finds the same in mine. Oh, well done. To
have shrunk that canker. It lacks but the one dimension,
your trick.

Magus   . . . Servant, sir.

Faustus   Cleanse it from memory.

Pause.

Magus   Give me but time.

Faustus   Bravo. Bravo, sir. Well said.

The **Wife** *again appears.*

Faustus   One moment. Here's a worthy adversary, which
is to say, companion . . . godlike, makes matter dissipate, the
savant smile with content . . .

The **Friend** *comes over to* **Faustus** *and whispers to him.*

Faustus   Yes, aid her. With thanks.

The **Friend** *and the* **Wife** *exit, leaving* **Faustus** *and the* **Magus**.

Faustus   With the one word. You win me to your cause,
I abjure philosophy and embrace prestidigitation. Where do
we part? Each utters a meaningless phrase to allow the mass
to ascribe to them a power not their own. In your case,
thaumaturgy, in mine, wisdom. Another effect.

The **Magus** *takes out a large silk.*

Faustus   No – improvise . . .

Magus   Direct me.

Faustus   Cure me my autumn cold.

Magus   Are you unwell?

Faustus   But with the change of season.

Magus   Take to your bed, and meditate upon a yellow
light.

Faustus   Shall I be thus cured?

Magus   Within the quarter-hour. But you in no event must
allow your mind freedom from this curative fluorescence.
One-tenth, one-twentieth second of impertinence, the cure is
null. And the disease shall worsen.

Faustus   Unto death?

Magus   Unless your will be of the strongest, I would forgo
the test.

Faustus   Physician-philosopher. May we suppose your
powers have no end?

Magus   Try me.

Faustus   What is the engine of the world?

Magus   The engine of the world's regret.

Faustus   Then, as you are a magus, proof me from it.

Magus   Here is a sovereign talisman against regret: never do that which might engender it.

Faustus   Oh, best of magicians. Are you then skilled to banish all disruption?

Magus   Sir, on the instant.

The **Magus** *prepares to perform a magical pass.*

The **Wife** *and the* **Friend** *enter.*

Magus   Watch here.

Wife   Faustus.

Faustus   Of course. Sir: with my apologies, to stunt your effect.

Magus   Your servant.

Faustus   And here take my leave – but with the one question.

Magus   Please . . .

Faustus   Where is the newspaper?

Magus   Sir, it is gone.

Faustus   Can matter be annihilated?

Magus   Alas.

Faustus   No, but reveal me the trick.

Magus   My revelation could not bring delight.

Faustus   May I not judge?

Magus   In my profession, as in yours, that given free must be despised.

Faustus   Indeed?

Magus   It is the one sure, certain law of life.

Faustus   Name me your forfeit.

Magus   Your respect, for I am asked to do that which can but cause disillusion.

Faustus   You have my respect. I swear it.

Magus (*magically producing the newspaper.*)   *Ecco* –

Faustus *takes the newspaper.*

Faustus   But this is not the gazette. The page is blank . . .

Wife   The child is unwell.

Faustus   He is but overset.

Wife   Yes.

Friend   Must we annul the entertainment?

Wife   Come with me now, Faustus. Enough.

Faustus   One moment, while I close with the jester. (*To* **Friend**.) Would you fetch my purse?

Friend (*as he hands* **Faustus** *a purse*)   Here is mine.

Faustus (*as he hands a sheet of paper to his* **Friend**)   Thank you, please, and be so good as to return this page to my manuscript. You remark, it is the final page . . .

Friend   . . . great honor.

Faustus   Go with my wife. Do not fret for the child. Surfeit must be released. Heavy air weighs on the lungs, the storms discharge it.

The **Friend** *exits.*

Faustus (*to the* **Magus**)   Maestro, my pardon. Take this – (*Of the purse.*) and with my thanks, I would not for the world release you, but as you perceive . . .

Magus   Servant, sir.

Faustus   I pray but for the restoration of the gazette.

Magus   I beg your pardon?

Faustus   Where is the journal?

Magus   Sir, it is vanished.

Faustus   Quite. But where? Shall I turn my back?

Magus   Sir, I have made the incantation, and the component atoms of the subject article . . .

Faustus   Indeed, then, I must class myself with those who, doubtless, importune you to reveal the secrets of your worthy craft.

Magus   Would you, again, sir, trade delight for disillusionment . . . ?

Faustus   I do not seek delight, but restoration. I require the journal.

Magus   Sir, I am at a stand.

Faustus   Sir: did you have me swear? Did you tax me to swear?

Magus   I do not know how, in faith, I may unclothe my craft.

Faustus   Did you not have me mime a ceremony, to do just that?

Magus   Indeed, it was but to augment th' effect . . . 'tis not for the uninitiated . . .

Faustus   Oh. Do I transgress a magical divide? Do I encroach upon the netherworld . . . ? Shall I avert my unschooled gaze lest it be seared by the mysteries . . . ? Poor uninitiate, to wander, sightless in the sacred grove. Do I offend? I beg pardon; but have I not contracted for your energy? And now have you, as comes to any artist, o'erreached yourself? Must you renounce your excellence, and crawl to kennel like a beaten dog, your poor trick revealed? How unlike the omnipotent priest you impersonate. (*Pause.*) Have you not been paid? Why do you hesitate?

Magus   I held, sir, but the one moment to compose my thought. For onlookers, discovering an illusion, fall into self-contempt, and, indeed, oft, to anger. I strove but for a

happy way to effect the restoration. I assure you I intended
no disrespect. (*Of purse.*) You have over-rewarded me, who
did not, in fact, perform. If I, in my search for a graceful
exit, caused offense, I humbly beg your pardon. Please guard
this pledge of my sincerity. (*He restores the purse to* **Faustus**.)
The journal may be found beneath your feet.

The **Magus** *begins to exit.*

Faustus   Wait, friend, wait, I beg you hear me, though,
indeed, I have no merit to plead. I have, I second you,
traduced whatever claim upon your graciousness. And I have
mocked you. In giddy self-absorption. I have no excuse, and
can but beg your pardon.

Magus   I do not comprehend you, sir.

Faustus   Indeed you do – oh, stay, and forgive me. Wait,
while I delineate it. We had engaged you. To perform, who
bought your time, and owe you, in return, attention . . .

Magus   Not were my play to fail . . .

Faustus   In any case, civility. From which we may not be
exempted. I am in breach. And plead, not as your
contractor, but as one man to his like, you feign a god, and
I a philosopher. Forgive me. Who most completely regrets
his offense.

Pause.

Magus   It were above me to forgive you.

Faustus   Oh no, naught but our parity wipes the slate
clean.

Magus   None but you has the power to suggest it.

Faustus   Must that debar me from my suit?

Magus   You plead your right to waive preferment.

Faustus   I do.

Magus   And yet, I cannot waive my subordination.

Faustus   Oh, my friend. Which makes my gaffe the less excusable. I am ashamed of my intemperate speech and offer my sincere apology.

Pause.

Magus   You entice me to my better self.

Faustus   I ask your pardon.

Magus   Were I to forward but its simulacrum?

Faustus   Come, sir, finally, let us be friends. Shall we not be friends? Mired together, in this – what shall we say . . . ? *Aid* me . . . in . . . ?

Magus   In a dark wood.

Faustus   In this underworld. Which you and I know as the world's nickname. Two philosophers, two showmen, seeking to astound, are we not?

Magus   You, sir, through your perception, I through trickery . . .

Faustus   Each, though, libel to frightened slander. Do I tax the conceit? My yokemate, as we pull the world on?

Magus   You o'er flatter me . . .

Faustus   As we: reason and folly, two paired oxen, wrestle the wagon of the world . . . ah, you smile, and now, encouraged by your approbation, having tapped its depth shall I now try its elasticity? Where did I leave my burden?

Magus   In a dark wood . . .

Faustus   In the dark wood, yes, our rough conveyance, fast in the mire, no purchase, night coming on . . .

Magus   You have neglected the storm.

Faustus   I stipulate it per tradition. And the cart, aid me, my friend.

Magus   Upon whose side we daub the name humanity . . .

Faustus   O precious perishable cargo . . . left to the strength . . .

Magus   Abandoned to the faltering strength . . .

Faustus   Of its mismatched beasts of travail: philosophy and magic . . . its castrated fattened cattle: Amuse me from this wood, O Magus. From this dark wood. From loneliness, my brother. O poor souls – who would begrudge us our self-pity – alone empowered, are we not?

Magus   Are we, sir?

Faustus   Possessors of that Secret Knowledge. And unable to discharge the burden.

Magus   To the which end, the paired oxen must pull together.

Faustus   There you are, my friend. A meeting in the dark wood. For it doth turn a burden, now and then . . .

Magus   In any pursuit . . .

Faustus   I would imagine, the uncertainty, the need to please . . .

Magus   Recurring, periodic self-doubt, sir, as we, increasing, master the few tricks, and, daily, doubt their worth.

Faustus   You speak, sir, for the company.

Pause.

Magus   Who drives your figure?

Faustus   Eh?

Magus   You speak of the oxen, and their cart . . . who is it directs them?

Faustus   Ah, yes, whom may we say? Who is the goad?

Magus   Perhaps, the family . . .

Faustus   The family.

Magus Perhaps one toils for their comfort, their safety and education.

Faustus Perhaps.

Magus Is it not so?

Faustus Though oft in our secret selves, we indict them, do we not?

Magus Indict them, you say, sir?

Faustus For their claim upon us.

Magus A legitimate claim.

Faustus How much the more oppressive?

Magus When is a man content?

Faustus I ask you. When may one be content? When work, and admiration, family, fame, nay, and *posterity* continually importune for acknowledgment. What poor conflicted souls. Who falsely name their pursuit 'liberty'.

Magus What is its secret name?

Pause.

Faustus Revenge. Those with whom I contend are phantoms. Those I instruct fools, or e'er either to avoid, or e'er applaud the obvious. I fear failure, I sicken of success, my sinews set in the mold in which work has stiffened them. I am unfitted even to unbend. I beg thee, brother, purge my soul of its self-content, show me the upper world, and I will follow. Poor, petted Faustus implores thee.

Magus I scarce know how to take you, sir.

Faustus No, no, induct me. Blister my flesh upon the candle, cause me to proffer oaths.

Magus What oaths?

Faustus Whate'er is traditional . . .

Offstage cries are heard.

Magus   The child cries.

Faustus   Its cries will cease. Shrive me. Bid me renounce th' immaterial world. I regret my preferment and beg for the chance to begin anew.

Magus   Ah: that is a plea I recognize.

Faustus   Then pity me. Ultimate physician.

Magus   Another bears that name.

Faustus   Perhaps you are his servant?

Magus   All are within his thrall.

Faustus   Indeed?

Magus   Is there not said to be salvation?

Faustus   Who returns to demonstrate it? (*Pause.*) What powers shall we importune?

Magus   I cede to you the choice.

Faustus   Teach me a trick.

Magus   I shall reveal a trick, in fact, the greatest of illusions.

The **Magus** *prepares to perform a magical flourish.*

The **Friend** *appears.*

Friend   Faustus.

Magus   . . . Behold.

Friend   Your wife sends to summon you.

Faustus   It is the child.

Friend   It is.

Magus   May all its trials be transient.

Faustus   It cries from excitement. It cries for a bruise at play. Its cries are sweet, for it may be comforted.

Friend   Your wife bids you attend immediately. (*Pause.*) Faustus.

Faustus (*to the* **Magus**)   Sir, I would not for the world, again, offend you. But, as you see. Sadly, as you see.

Magus   Of course.

Faustus (*to the* **Friend**)   I come on the instant.

The **Friend** *exits.*

Faustus (*to the* **Magus**)   My thanks, sir, from the heart, for your companionship. I forestall, until that day, the renewed delight of our continued brotherhood.

Magus   You asked to be taught a trick.

Faustus   I must plead a postponement.

Magus   E'en to discover the most complete effect?

Faustus   I do not doubt your skill. Howe'er, my duties abrogate even your power, O Magus, to transfix me. Servant, sir.

Faustus *starts to depart.*

Magus   Your manuscript contains an error.

Faustus (*pause*)   What?

Magus   As I have said.

Faustus   Ah. Yes. Well done. My manuscript. An overheard exchange prompts an improvisation. A misplaced punctuation mark, an orthographic fault.

Magus   It hides an error which, to posterity, serves to nullify the work entire.

Faustus   Have you then seen the future?

Magus   It is one with the past.

Faustus   Absent the provoking generalities.

Magus   Do you challenge me?

Faustus   I do. What do you know of my philosophy?

Magus   'Tis said you are like Adam, before whom were brought all God's creation, and whate'er he chose to call them, so they were called. And now you are complete. Your long years' journey summarized in mathematical perfection.

Faustus   You speak of my new work?

Magus   I do.

Faustus   I penned the last page but this afternoon.

Magus   You wish me to quote it to you.

Faustus   I do.

Magus   'Wherein we find that number . . .'

Faustus   No . . .

Magus   Indeed, 'is not, and signifies not a quantity, but a progression.' Shall I continue? Shall I quote the formula?

Friend (*entering*)   Faustus.

Faustus   Stop. He has purloined the manuscript.

Friend   Faustus, the child cries . . .

Faustus   Are you a thief?

Magus   I am not.

Faustus   Then how have you divined my thesis's burden?

Magus   I cannot debase my trade to the uninitiated.

Faustus   Is it then, mere manipulation?

Magus   That is the charge I must withhold.

Faustus   Who bids you? Are you a *spy*?

Magus   I assure you I am not.

Faustus   Are you a telepath, sir? No, then I say you are a thief . . .

Friend   Faustus . . .

Faustus   . . . one moment.

The **Friend** *exits.*

Faustus   Ah, well done. I had insulted you, and wronged
your craft. And though we kissed rings must you not have
your revenge. And, now, you have had your revenge . . .
Now you have bested me. Now we may cry quits. Now. You
quote my conclusions in my actual language. This is an
effect which –

Magus   But if it is not an effect –

Faustus   You vex me with fooling, sir. Howe'er you call it,
effect, illusion, nay, a miracle. Induct me, but for the one
circumstance. I will not reveal your art. I plead not from
mere curiosity, but from material concern. For the security
of my work, of my manuscript . . .

Magus   But what if the manuscript . . . were to contain a
fault?

Faustus   Please.

Magus   Grant it hypothetically.

Faustus   Is that your precondition?

Magus   What if your manuscript contained a disqualificatory
error?

Pause.

Faustus   I would amend it.

Magus   And if to do so were to unpick its essential fibre . . .
(*Pause.*) To unsay the work entire . . . ?

Faustus   I cannot imagine such a fault.

Magus   But if such were revealed to you . . . a fault which
were, to all succeeding ages, to cast your work as a byword
and a jest.

Faustus   Instance an example of such error.

Magus   If it were stolen from another.

Pause.

Faustus   But it is not.

Magus   But if it were. That would, of course, set it as an example of that error which might not be put aright.

Faustus   Deservedly.

Magus   If it were purloined.

Faustus   Yes.

Magus   In whole or part.

Faustus   As I have said. Thus?

Magus   You asked me to instance a category of error. I have done so.

Faustus   Yes, there's your small casuistic victory. I grant the category. My work, however, is unblemished.

Magus   So you say.

Faustus   I do.

Magus   But would you swear an oath?

Faustus   I do not follow you, sir.

Magus   Indeed you do, but cannot overtake me . . . You press me to reveal the occult. To protect, as you say, the sanctity of your creation, you ask me to unclothe my own. I reply: swear it is yours entire.

Faustus   It is.

Magus   Upon your family. (*Pause.*) And yet you will not assert it.

Faustus   The thoughtful hesitate to take an oath.

Magus   The thoughtful.

Faustus   It is from a sense of probity.

Magus   Not from fear . . . ?

Faustus   I think not.

Magus As who would say 'I swear on my life,' or 'on my children's life' . . .

Faustus But who would proffer such an oath?

Magus What is the risk?

Faustus Not risk, but impropriety. As who would sully the name of his wife, say, in a tavern; of his children, in the street. These practices are private, not to be profanely uttered.

Magus And yet we swear to God, and account it a jest.

Faustus With respect, this is a disquisition not on the notional Dark Forces, but on the vagaries of language.

Magus Ah, language is all.

Faustus The cries of birds may communicate some little-more-than-instinct, one to the next, but are to the higher order, nothing more than song. As must our plaintive imprecations be to those chimerical powers above.

Magus And yet we hesitate before them.

Faustus Again, what does it signify?

Magus That is my question, sir, to you.

Faustus I swear the work is mine.

Magus Upon your family.

Faustus Were I proved in default.

Magus . . . By whom?

Faustus I swear the work is of my invention complete, entire.

Magus Upon the lives of your wife and child.

Faustus Tell how you knew of my formula.

Magus I will not reveal myself to one unbound. Will you swear? (*Pause.*) Will you swear?

Pause.

Faustus   I will.

Magus   Upon the dirk. (*He draws the dirk and holds it in front of* **Faustus**.) Grasp it.

Faustus *takes the dirk.*

Faustus   I swear upon the lives of my wife and child. The manuscript is mine entire. Are you content? Am I now sworn?

Magus   You are.

Faustus   Then divulge to me how you came to know of my work's conclusion.

Magus   I overheard your shortsighted friend, muttering the phrases to himself as he perused it. Now see my poor magic's operation, and trade consternation for contempt. Do you despise me?

Faustus   Howe'er that may be. Good day, sir. I must take my leave.

Magus   Is time so short?

Faustus   My child . . .

Magus   You note his cries have ceased.

Faustus   Which need not trouble you. Adieu.

Magus   But tarry.

Faustus *starts toward the upstage doors to his home.*

Faustus   My family bids me.

Magus   They have no more need of you. They are long dead. You are forsworn, and your false oath has consigned them to Hell.

The **Magus** *gestures, we hear the far-off ringing of a bell. The doors blow open violently to reveal a scene of gray desolation, remnants of a building, a low mist upon the ground.*

Faustus turns from looking at the scene, to confront the **Magus**, *whom, we find, has vanished.*

Act Two

The portals which led to **Faustus**'s *home are opened, to reveal an expanse, upstage, of gray ruin.*

Faustus *comes on to the stage, and looks around him. We hear a far-off bell ringing, and see an old man walking in the ruins.*
Faustus *turns to encounter him. We see it is his* **Friend***, Fabian, now greatly aged.*

Faustus Where do we find ourselves?

Friend I've often thought that it is Hell.

Faustus In truth?

Friend I am grown so old it nor diverts nor profits me to lie.

Faustus Have you grown old?

Friend As you observe.

Faustus But we are of an age.

Friend If you assert it.

Faustus Do you not know me?

Friend Your voice is not unfamiliar, but perhaps it merely pleases.

Faustus Turn to me, look on me.

Friend It would not profit, no, for I am blind.

Faustus Blind.

Friend Yes.

Faustus What has befallen you? How came you to age?

Friend Sir, I assure you, it was the passage of time.

Faustus (*pause*) Are you mad? (*Pause.*) Can you not answer me? Can you not aid me?

Friend Not the first, sir, but, perhaps, the second.

Faustus I do not understand.

Friend A sundial may offer information but, you remark, it withholds comment. (*Pause.*)

Faustus Do you not know me?

Friend I beg pardon.

Faustus I am Faustus.

Friend Ask again if I am mad, I shall return the favour.

Faustus You suggest the debility is mine?

Friend You have said that you are Faustus.

Faustus I am he.

Friend What sane being would assert it?

Faustus I do not understand.

Friend Then you are mad. (*He starts off.*) Or perverse, merely. I mean no offense. Whom could I dare offend?

Faustus Do not desert me.

Friend Aid me then. Would you oblige, in description of the scene?

Faustus Near the conjunction of two roads.

Friend I shall no further trouble you. (*He walks off.*)

Faustus Stay, for I am unmoored; the pawl has clicked, the wheel come round, but I am baffled by the revolution. I beg you. Fabian. What is this charade? I do not understand its nature.

Friend Nor I. Could I have creditably done so, would I not have resigned, long ago? But we understand, that is a crime, for which the criminals, self-punished, are additionally damned. And their bones to an unmarked grave, at a crossroads.

Faustus   Do I dream?

Friend   Should you, then I felicitate you.

Faustus   Where is the family of Faustus?

Friend   Do I in fact remark your voice, sir? Or is it but th' association, summon'd by your questionings? But it is the same whate'er, and as the world draws in, as sight, sound, and action erode, what remains, but self-absorption? Where all is made fast to decay.

Faustus   How came this to be so?

Friend   Through time and effort, as most things.

Faustus   But how? The house is vanished, you are aged, yet time has not passed.

Friend   Then how am I grown old?

Faustus   Indeed, who are but one day older than we found you yesterday.

Friend   Bless you, I must accept it, but, yesterday, I was old. I was old and blind.

Faustus   You have gone blind from drink.

Friend   Thanks, good physician. But the cause was ne'er in doubt. (*Pause.*) I wondered at the cure, though, those years. Till it grew plain, you see, like a far-off disturbing shape, which, upon approach, resolves itself, until we say, 'tis but a fault in the treeline.

Faustus   And it resolved, to you, the cure for your disease?

Friend   'Twas, of course, death. Which occupied decades of schooling. But I was blessed in my exemplars.

Faustus   To wit?

Friend   I watched a family sicken and die, first the young lad, and then the woman, from grief. As she cried, over the years, for wisdom, then for fortitude, and, as any invalid, for this or that drug, in the hope it offered hope, till it was burned out of her.

Faustus   Say on.

Friend   Her beauty, her desire, even for understanding, ebbed, till she was like the hollow tree, which at length falls, of which we say, how not to've remarked, it died long ago. On the one hand, she had a long life. On the other, poor angel, she lived it anguished.

Faustus   Where is the family lives here?

Friend   They have preceded us.

Faustus   A prosperous family once controlled the land.

Friend   They own it still, though somewhat less of it. Perhaps you'd aid me, sir, to seek that freehold.

Faustus   Whose grave do you seek?

Friend   It were a crime, they say, to name it.

Faustus   The boy.

Friend   The boy?

Faustus   Faust's son.

Friend   Bless you, no, sir.

Faustus   Then tell me he lives.

Friend   To please you, sir, I will. But in effect his crypt lies yonder.

Faustus   His crypt.

Friend   Untended these long years.

Faustus   Not by his mother . . . ?

Pause.

Friend   One may not speak of her.

Faustus   Why?

Friend   Have I not told you?

Pause.

Faustus   Do you say she is dead?

Friend   You will forgive me, sir, my thoughts, absent direction, take their own lead.

Faustus   Where is the woman's grave?

Friend   One may not know, sir, the grave of a suicide, who are damned to Hell. Do you feign ignorance of that gentle law? It extends e'en to those fair angels, on the earth, e'en those whose being cleansed and chastened. Whose each movement spoke of patience and grace, who were the anodyne to a life of dull disappointment, in whose very existence one found comfort for the, will I say, cruel impossibility of her possession. Fair, wasted angel. Self-slain, ne'er consummated love. O distance and O blessed death. Shall I requite your queries, sir? Those who impertinently usurp the divine, rest in an unmarked grave. What matter. When eternity wastes all.

Faustus   Some say God is immortal.

Friend   Some say the sinful dead writhe in perpetual torment.

Faustus   How did the boy die?

Friend   In an ague. Taken in a cold night. In a vain and protracted search for another. In despair, at his abandonment.

Faustus   Abandonment, you say.

Friend   By the man.

Faustus   You will not say his name?

Friend   He died in grief, at his father's disappearance. It is a difficulty, as you may come to know, in age, to guard an undiminished hatred. After a time. That which once burned as molten iron. Becomes a mere fixed habit of the mind. Till one wakes one day, to find its very exercise an enervation.

Faustus Hatred.

Friend Yes. But some does not die.

Faustus Must not all feeling change with time?

Friend The truly wronged know otherwise.

Faustus Who has wronged you?

We hear the sound of a bell, and the man starts off.

Friend I must go, for he hunts for me. Do you not find, we feel most beholden, sir, to those supplying an unnecessary service . . . ?

Faustus Who wronged you?

Friend Who, indeed? He whom we indulged. To our cost. Our petted philosopher – who burned with the thirst for truth. Who betrayed those who trusted him, parsing their love to tribute and then to oblivion. Our sick creation. False friend, inconstant husband, engorged obscene digest of self-reference. We nurtured, for the entertainment, for the reflected glory – for which we shall not be forgiven. Who abided him, who, in his diffidence, subjected those he loved first to danger, then, to destruction, as I watched. I might have acted. I feared reproof, and classed it as respect for the proprieties. 'Twas not he, then, but I, sir, as you see, who was the criminal – to have subjected them to him. I must go. (*He starts off.*)

Faustus Stay: may I beg a service?

Friend From one unfit as myself?

Faustus Where does she lie?

Friend Act as I. Elect a spot, devote your obsequies, pray that it is her grave.

The **Friend** *starts off.*

Faustus (*to the departing* **Friend**) No, it offends sense. Say the man vanished, would not his family first misdoubt, accident, or illness, a man so beloved.

Friend   He fled in cowardice. Who would not brave public ridicule.

Faustus   Ridicule?

Friend   Of his mis-envisioned, uncompleted work.

Faustus   Uncompleted . . . ?

We hear the bell. The **Friend** *goes off.*

Faustus   Am I unmanned to've lost the basic rudiments of reason?

The **Magus** *appears onstage, carrying a large book.*

Faustus   Where is my family? (*Pause.*) I have addressed you, sir.

Magus   I've noted it.

Faustus   Where is my family?

Magus   As is the destiny of all seed, they have been dispersed.

Faustus   By what authority?

Magus   The less evolved would enquire by what mechanism. Good.

Faustus   It is an illusion.

Magus   What is not? As have you not thrilled to teach us?

Faustus   It is delusion, it is mesmeric projection, I lack the term to name the method, the motive is plain.

Magus   To wit?

Faustus   A vicious act of envy. I have detractors, as must any prominent man. Indeed, I must have enemies. Have they employed you to drive me mad? To play upon my doubts? Have they told you of my shortcomings? Of my pride, of my unchecked imagination? Are you a tool of enmity? Of spite? Are you that inevitable assassin the elevated must fear, whose lack they themselves supply in

counterpoise to their election . . . ? Are you madness . . . ?
What are you? I conjure you . . .

Magus   By what? I shall not press you.

Faustus   Damn your impertinence, sir, and damn your
illusion. I demand that you cease, restore, and revert all
various aspects of the pantomime. The joke pales shockingly.
And farewell, now farewell. Name and receive your payment,
sir, for this diversion.

Magus   I have both named and received it.

Faustus   It is a trick.

Magus   Pray accept this in compensation.

He hands **Faustus** *the volume he has been holding in his hands.*
Faustus *takes it.*

Faustus   What pretends this to be?

Magus   It is your manuscript.

Faustus   But it is aged . . .

Magus   . . . indeed . . .

Faustus *takes the book and reads.*

Faustus   'A discovery of the philosophic principles of
periodicity . . .'

He continues to leaf through the book.

The book is aged.

Magus   It is.

Faustus   My friend, also, and decayed. (*Pause.*) That which
appears to be the remnant of my home bespeaks a passage
of years.

Magus   From which you conclude? (*Pause.*)

Faustus   Where is my family?

Magus   Yes? Are you frightened?

Faustus   Show them to me.

Magus   They are dead, you have murdered them.

Faustus   Strong, striking verbiage, yet hardly discourse. You recur to causality. Then I have you, sir. For name me the system of philosophy, or physics wherein effect may be without cause. For what freak do you suppose to punish me? Respond. I charge you.

Magus   You made a wager.

Faustus   A wager? That is your plea? You rest the destruction of my happiness upon a bet? Oh, the wronged, are ever disadvantaged in debate. For the aggressor may assert now this, now that, unfettered by fact, truth, or history. While the betrayed –

Magus   No more betrayed, but called to account. You contracted a wager.

Faustus   I repudiate it.

Magus   One may repudiate the payment but of that which one holds in possession. Else it is called 'chagrin'.

Faustus   Then I defy you, parse me the wager, sir, in justice.

Magus   But we delighted. To revile the advocates of justice; how we decried as puerile those who served; reason, and tradition, custom, law . . . Your work, your discourse, and, in fact, your life were dedicated to the abrogation of commonalities.

Faustus   Is it for this I am punished?

Magus   You are not punished, but foreclosed.

Faustus   Then save me the gloss, and assert the forfeit. By your terms, sir, by your terms.

Magus   I will not foul the laws of fair debate.

Faustus   So you have said. Then show me the default, sir, or restore all.

Magus   I name your magnum opus.

Faustus (*as he holds up the book*)   It survives.

Magus   You still seek fame?

Faustus   Yes, I am arrogant. Nay, arrogance itself, spare me the lesson. My work survives. You asserted it contained a flaw.

Magus   I did.

Faustus   Indeed, a theft, which would disqualify it from renown save as a jest. A fool, a vicious and unwarranted asseveration.

Magus   Which, were it to be established . . .

Faustus   . . . I complete, which, were it proved supportable, would, would, would. (*Pause.*) You taunted me. You dared me, as I understood, to take an oath. I took it as a jest.

Magus   You swore to the false, that which you staked was forfeit.

Faustus   That my work was purloined? I defy you, sir, to suggest my work the subject of . . . yes, say, yes, incomprehension, yes, but impossibly of scorn. Let us grant you the passage of time. I cede you the truth of your illusion. Does my work not survive? (*He holds up the book.*)

Magus   But as a curio.

Faustus   A *curio*? I call you to render justice.

Magus   Justice is blind, you have said she is also deaf.

Faustus   But you are neither. You structure your chicanery in the mechanic mode: if this, then that. Then *habeas deleatur:* show me the fault.

Magus (*of the book*)   Read.

Faustus   I am acquainted with it – I composed it. 'Tis mine entire. You charge me as a plagiarist. Show me the fault. I defy you.

Magus   Turn to the end.

Faustus (*turns to the end*)   Indeed I shall.

Magus   Turn the last leaf and read.

Faustus   Yes, yes, it is the final formula, and the apotheosis of the argument, where number is revealed but as progression.

Magus   Yes.

Faustus   You feign I am undone in the conclusion? That it is debarred as purloined? It cannot be purloined, for it is pure imagination.

Magus   Turn the leaf.

Faustus *does so.*

Faustus   What viciousness is this? (*Reads.*)

> 'Three swift swallows in the summer sky,
> Gone in the twinkling of an eye.
> One for the heart, one for the head,
> One for the lad who tarries abed.'

Pause.

It is the child's poem.

Magus   The manuscript appears under your name. Yet, you deny the conclusion's authorship.

Faustus   The poem. How found it its way into my composition?

Magus   Take the page from your tunic. And read.

Faustus *does so and reads:*

Faustus   ' . . . that number signifies not a quantity, but a progression . . .' This is not forfeit, sir, but mere prestidigitation.

Magus   Ah, sir, do you now conceive the world as a balance? Must one not then suppose one to read the scale?

Which supposition you have dedicated your life, nay, in fact, this work, to disprove?

Faustus   What power sends you as a plague, or are you an excrudescence of the general theme? Of envy. (*Pause.*) What of my family?

Magus   They ran the extended limit of their course. They died. They perhaps continue, in a parallel world. As before. As e'er we ever met. Say it is true. Take comfort, and believe it.

Faustus   Is it true?

Magus   Is it true? And you transfigured, from our brave savant into a missish postulate who wished to know: the weight of the world, the run of time, the final construction of matter . . . as the poor fool who wished to understand grief. Your wish has been granted.

Faustus   I could not have foreseen.

Magus   *Truly . . . ?* Then you should not have spoke. Or have your vaunted experiments in science taught you to pray that cause has no effect?

Faustus   I understand. That I've offended, in some wise, or you, or, say if I go amiss, or, say, a tradition, or a power you represent. I pray to you to accept my regrets, and teach me how to particularise my homage. How shall I address you?

Magus   Well begun. Call me a merchant.

Faustus   What do you seek?

Magus   As any merchant. That which in my realm is scarce.

Faustus   What have you brought?

Magus   Say I have brought you fire.

Faustus   Will not the gods be angry?

Magus   Suppose it their constant state.

Pause.

Faustus   From whence do you come?

Magus   Shall you know more when I have told you?

Faustus   Fit the response to my understanding.

Magus   Say from the future. Or the past. Say from another realm.

Faustus   I am afraid.

Magus   You balked at the transmutation of a card. As the rock-dwelling savages recoiled at fire. You conflate number, speech, thought, the mental and physical, and call your work complete. You are unfit e'en to frame the problem as a dog to speak; it lacks the mechanism.

Pause.

Faustus   Sir . . . (*Pause.*) Sir . . . Ah, sir. Ah, good sir. Ah worthy preceptor, to school in atonement. To strip from me, the prop of self-regard. To offer that omnipotent admixture of grief and self-humiliation . . .

Magus   Whom do you think confronts you? (*Pause.*) You hesitate.

Faustus   Yes.

Magus   From confusion?

Faustus   No. No, from . . .

Pause.

Magus   You must supply the word.

Faustus   From awe.

Pause.

Magus   I attend . . .

Pause.

Faustus   We have heard voices. In the dark. In childhood, in extremity. Perhaps at death . . . we have construed them as . . . (*Pause.*) those promptings religion derogates as survival of savagery. Of ancient, superseded nature . . .

Magus   The power of which you speak. Does it possess a name?

Faustus   What do you want of me?

Magus   I await your suggestion.

Faustus   No, the gods would damn me, can it be, for the ignorance of a formula?

Magus   Upon what then, should they rely?

Faustus   Upon . . . upon the evidence, say of my contrition.

Magus   What leads you to believe they prefer it to the entertainment of your pain?

Faustus   I cannot credit it.

Magus   Are they, then, in contradistinction to your avowed thesis, omniscient and benign?

Faustus   My works are empty, I abjure them. They are the toy of an overfed mind.

Magus   Truly?

Faustus   I have been wrong. In which I am but human. God spare me. My life was not without merit.

Magus   What merit might that be?

Faustus   My family . . . My wife loved me, my child.

Magus   He loved you?

Faustus   He penned me a poem.

Magus   Did you not derogate it?

Faustus   Did I? Then may God forgive me.

Magus   Read it to me . . .

Faustus   . . . Why?

Magus   To conflate the two.

Faustus   I confess, the two productions are one, my manuscript, and the child's poem. Yes. I am taught. His is superior.

Magus   Why?

Faustus   His . . . His was writ in love. I . . .

Magus   Confess –

Faustus   I . . . shall confess . . . to my petted self-adoration. To coward miching, to entertainment of the establishment which I was licensed to decry. I was a whore, corrupt for all time, and unfit for any purpose greater than debauchery.

Magus   You divert, but fail to convince of your sincerity. Confess.

Faustus   To what end?

Magus   To the end that you cease to enquire, for my entertainment, for no end at all.

Faustus   God help me.

Magus   God spare me, the frightened call, and confect endless, elaborate self-castigation. Spared, they employ reprieve in sin. Thus coupling cowardice to comedy.

Faustus   Until . . . ?

Magus   Shall we turn to the coda? Shall we exhibit those upon whom you practised your charade? Shall we show you your family?

Faustus   You have said they are dead.

Magus   As if they never lived, or dwelt, solely in your imagination. (*Pause.*) Or the imagination of another.

Faustus   Of what other?

Magus   Shall I tell you?

Pause.

Faustus   Show me my family.

Magus   Your son's in heaven, and beyond my sway.

Faustus   My wife?

Magus   She is damned as a suicide – with *her* you may be reunited.

Faustus   Yes, I see.

Magus   So you perceive the tariff.

Pause.

Faustus   Sir, you have seduced me, you have played upon my weakness. You indict me of hypocrisy, of greed, of self-blind egoism; your victory makes good your claim. You now taunt me with cowardice. Where I confront you. I wish to see my wife.

Magus   Nothing may be had for nothing.

Faustus   Yes, merchant – yes, I see that for which you have come. I close the bargain. And am shed of you. Give me the dagger.

Magus   In truth, sir, then you do impress.

Faustus   Indeed I care not. Give me the knife.

The **Magus** *hands* **Faustus** *the dirk. The* **Magus** *retires upstage, leaving* **Faustus** *alone, as the doors close.*

Faustus   Omnipotent winter which alone reveals the underlying structure of the land – he who has sought beauty in the ruined, how otherwise than reap this empty, sad, perpetual requital. Who sickens to the point where wisdom lies with the ironmonger. Here is damnation, then. And there's an end to hypocrisy . . .

He puts the knife to his throat. Upstage the doors blow open to reveal Hell, from which we see appear **Faustus**'s **Wife**, *in torn, soot-blackened garments. Pause. As* **Faustus** *looks at his* **Wife**:

Faustus   My wife, my angel wife.

Faustus *hesitates. The* **Magus** *appears at his side.*

Magus   You may continue.

Faustus   How may I frame my contrition? . . . For what may I beg . . . ?

Magus   For pardon . . . ?

Faustus   May I beg for pardon?

Magus   You hesitate.

Faustus   I would not waste the least of her attention. I beg the one moment to compose the speech.

Magus   It makes no odds, as she cannot hear. We to her are less than phantoms.

Pause.

Wife   It is an adamantine monument. To sin for surely it must be the fruit of crime, though what I know not, to have elected that course which concludes in such calamity. Or were it better never to have lived? Or spent a life barren and envious. For could not envy be borne? You were envious. Your theme was covetousness – and self-worship.

Faustus   Whom does she address?

Magus   As you suspect.

Wife   You envied all fame but your own, and basked in the self-awarded mantle of simplicity. And we who loved, indulged you. To your cost. As the petted dog pierces our assumed severity. He understands innocuous chastisement as praise. And seeks it. By soiling his home. You strove for fame. For the delusion of popular love. My son, my son, sacrifice to a profligate, absconding father . . . And I chose you. Fool, wicked fool. Perpetually damned mother − for what sin was I coupled to you in penance? Unnatural vicious father. How odd. When devotion engulfed you.

Faustus My wife.

Wife This is a mother's plaint. Formed as a fugue: of pride and fear, regret and uncertainty. It is the most ancient song of conquest. For women conquer but the once, and then are self-schooled. Poor story. To live supine. First to conceive, and then to bear. At long last only licensed to revolve, our face to the ground. But to weep. (*We hear the pealing of the bell.*) . . . Yes, I attend . . .

Magus See how the circularity augments the grief.

Wife Fool woman who was content with little. With so little . . . (*The* **Wife** *exits.*)

Magus Indeed, dashing all barriers to its intensification. The dropped stone stops at earth, gluttony brings repletion, the libertine copulates but to debility, in each the cure grows apace with the malady. It is a law. In all things but grief.

Faustus Grief must find a rest.

Magus Behold the exception. She is a suicide, and lives for ever. A self-perpetuating energy, increased in moment through sheer force of contemplation. Must we not stand unabashed, to receive whate'er of insight, awe, or entertainment our various natures may propose.

Faustus God damn you.

Magus Blasphemy and prayer are one. An appeal, thus an assertion of a superior power. Do you acknowledge it? I ask. Do you, at length, sense the true meaning of confession?

Faustus I wish to see my son.

Magus You have bartered and been paid.

Faustus I call upon God . . .

Magus And I invite you to denounce God.

Faustus   I denounce the Devil, in all of his undertakings.
I convict myself, of a life of heresy. My every thought
idolatrous, all my devotions sham, and homage to a false
god. I disclaim them, I renounce every thought, exhortation,
observance, devotion, and deed as sin and prostrate myself,
helpless, before the One True God. It cannot lack precedent.
Grant me the power to frame my contrition. Dear God,
hear my prayer.

Magus   Why should a god prefer your prayers to your
agony?

Faustus   Let that stand as my offering: the anguish of a
contrite heart. I beg for recision of my child's death, of my
wife's suffering. God, who can read my heart, mighty judge,
with no deeds to plead for him, here stands your servant,
shriven, at last, to your will. Hear me.

Magus   The voices of the Damned may not be heard
above.

Faustus   I then plead for an intercessor. To one consecrated
to Heaven. To speak for me. I call upon my son. My son,
an angel.

Magus   Do not name him.

Faustus   Then there exists that intuited mercy. Yes. To
which your speech testifies. My son, untouched by sin,
unimplicated, blameless. Is there not that bond? Stronger
than death – a sweet, unending child's love. O son, say that
you hear my prayer.

The drop parts behind **Faustus** *now to reveal Heaven, where we find*
Faustus's *son.*

Boy   I hear you . . .

Faustus *turns to see his son, and advances to him.*

Faustus   O blessed child, how the sweet moment stuns me
to chastisement. Dear child. O son of my heart, exult the
power which vouchsafed this interview. O son, intercede for
me.

Boy   Intercede . . .

Faustus   For a poor penitent. Who implores your forgiveness. Plead for me, not for my worth, I have none. For yours. Forward your merit in my case. Bear my petition.

Boy   Ah, that is why you have appeared today.

Faustus   . . . today.

Boy   Today is the day of atonement.

Faustus   . . . of atonement.

Boy   You bear a petition.

Faustus   I do.

Boy   Say it to me.

Faustus   Yes, I shall – my angel – that my wife, that my child, and myself may return, to the earth, whole, and restored, as before.

Boy   Whole and restored.

Faustus   Bear my plea. Best of the two worlds. Through all my criminal confusion one truth endured, undoubted, and pure. That of your love – pity me, and preach your benignity in my cause on high.

Boy   I shall.

Faustus   Praise God – oh, praise God.

Boy   But to plead in the cause of whom?

Pause.

Faustus   Can you not know me?

Boy   How should I know you? (*Pause.*) Am I not endless blessed?

Faustus   You are.

Boy   In what could eternal blessing consist save in oblivion?

Pause.

Faustus   . . . My son.

Boy   Am I your son?

Faustus   Surely there's a residuary memory. An ineradicable memory.

Boy   Of?

Faustus   Of love. Between a father and son. Which transcends death. I know it. In my soul. It is an attribute of God. Our love.

Boy   And did I love you?

Faustus   Oh, my son.

Boy   Tell me of love.

Faustus   . . . No, can you doubt me?

Boy   I am unfitted to perceive duplicity. I ask as for a gift.

Faustus   Yes, I shall tell you of love.

Boy   In this particular: the better to fit me to plead your case. It is the hour of audience.

Faustus   Yes.

Boy   When the bell toll, and until the bell cease. And the gates have closed.

Faustus   A man, a family begs to be reunited. In love . . . you wrote of it.

Boy   Tell me.

Faustus   You wrote a poem. You composed me a poem. Bear it on high. Attend:

'Heavy, heavy the hired man
Weary, how weary the willing hand . . .'

Boy   But this is a sad recital.

Faustus   'Tis but the preamble.

Boy   It awakens memory.

Faustus   Yes.

Boy   But, 'tis memory of pain.

Faustus   Of pain . . .

Boy   Yes . . .

Faustus   No, but let me continue.

Boy   'Tis a sad song.

Faustus   It turns. Wait . . . see: at the end . . .

Boy   You say it speaks of love.

Faustus   It does. Complete it for me. (*Pause.*) Why do you hesitate?

Pause. We hear a bell tolling.

I must go. It is the hour of intercession. Until the bell cease. Give me the poem, and it shall plead for you.

Faustus   Wait . . .

The **Child** *begins to disappear. The* **Magus** *appears.*

Faustus   Return me my book.

Magus   You have renounced it.

Faustus   Give me the poem.

Magus   You remark I bid you peruse it.

Faustus   I am summoned to approach the Throne.

Magus   And you are debarred. (*Pause.*) The biddable ape, whose antics delight in their travesty of understanding. His fist closed tight around the nut in the glass jar. He rallies Heaven for an explanation. He invokes his merit and his ancestry. See now his simian face contort in travesty of philosophic consternation. You wonder why you are pursued? For entertainment.

Faustus   I am to you but a diversion.

Magus   In fine.

Faustus   Then pay me.

Magus   Pay you?

Faustus   For the one thing's true, in Heaven or Hell, and by your own admission, one must pay for entertainment. Pay me, then, who has entertained you. Give me my poem. Give me my poem.

Magus   Who has vexed me since you first besought me.

Faustus *is handed the poem, and starts to leave.*

Faustus   I ne'er besought you, sir, my friend besought you.

Magus   I was summoned by your o'erweening pride.

Faustus   My pride . . .

Magus   And your impertinence.

Faustus   And have I not prevailed?

Magus   Then go boast of your victory. I tire of you.

Faustus   Or do you fear me?

Magus   Fear you . . .

Faustus   Or do I see, in your capitulation, a man taken at his word? His word ratified by the respect which attends his approach?

A bell rings.

Magus   The gates are closing.

Faustus   And that you, with your trumpery scorn, seek to dismiss him who had bested you. Who wrenched from you licence to see Heav'n and Hell and walk free. Who has probed the centre.

A bell rings.

Magus   . . . to have found . . . ?

Faustus   . . . the Secret Engine of the World. O sacred light, the signs congeal, you are come to induct me . . .

A bell rings.

Magus   The gates are closing.

Faustus   I am become as God.

Magus   And now the gates are closed.

Faustus   I am completed.

Magus   As, My Lord, am I.

Methuen Modern Plays

include work by

Edward Albee
Jean Anouilh
John Arden
Margaretta D'Arcy
Peter Barnes
Sebastian Barry
Brendan Behan
Dermot Bolger
Edward Bond
Bertolt Brecht
Howard Brenton
Anthony Burgess
Simon Burke
Jim Cartwright
Caryl Churchill
Noël Coward
Lucinda Coxon
Sarah Daniels
Nick Darke
Nick Dear
Shelagh Delaney
David Edgar
David Eldridge
Dario Fo
Michael Frayn
John Godber
Paul Godfrey
David Greig
John Guare
Peter Handke
David Harrower
Jonathan Harvey
Iain Heggie
Declan Hughes
Terry Johnson
Sarah Kane
Charlotte Keatley
Barrie Keeffe
Howard Korder

Robert Lepage
Doug Lucie
Martin McDonagh
John McGrath
Terrence McNally
David Mamet
Patrick Marber
Arthur Miller
Mtwa, Ngema & Simon
Tom Murphy
Phyllis Nagy
Peter Nichols
Sean O'Brien
Joseph O'Connor
Joe Orton
Louise Page
Joe Penhall
Luigi Pirandello
Stephen Poliakoff
Franca Rame
Mark Ravenhill
Philip Ridley
Reginald Rose
Willy Russell
Jean-Paul Sartre
Sam Shepard
Wole Soyinka
Shelagh Stephenson
Peter Straughan
C. P. Taylor
Theatre de Complicite
Theatre Workshop
Sue Townsend
Judy Upton
Timberlake Wertenbaker
Roy Williams
Snoo Wilson
Victoria Wood

Methuen Contemporary Dramatists

include

John Arden (two volumes)
Arden & D'Arcy
Peter Barnes (three volumes)
Sebastian Barry
Dermot Bolger
Edward Bond (six volumes)
Howard Brenton
   (two volumes)
Richard Cameron
Jim Cartwright
Caryl Churchill (two volumes)
Sarah Daniels (two volumes)
Nick Darke
David Edgar (three volumes)
Ben Elton
Dario Fo (two volumes)
Michael Frayn (three volumes)
David Greig
John Godber (two volumes)
Paul Godfrey
John Guare
Lee Hall (two volumes)
Peter Handke
Jonathan Harvey
   (two volumes)
Declan Hughes
Terry Johnson (two volumes)
Sarah Kane
Barrie Keefe
Bernard-Marie Koltès
David Lan
Bryony Lavery
Deborah Levy
Doug Lucie

David Mamet (four volumes)
Martin McDonagh
Duncan McLean
Anthony Minghella
   (two volumes)
Tom Murphy (four volumes)
Phyllis Nagy
Anthony Neilsen
Philip Osment
Louise Page
Stewart Parker (two volumes)
Joe Penhall
Stephen Poliakoff
   (three volumes)
David Rabe
Mark Ravenhill
Christina Reid
Philip Ridley
Willy Russell
Eric-Emmanuel Schmitt
Ntozake Shange
Sam Shepard (two volumes)
Shelagh Stephenson
Wole Soyinka (two volumes)
David Storey (three volumes)
Sue Townsend
Judy Upton
Michel Vinaver
   (two volumes)
Arnold Wesker (two volumes)
Michael Wilcox
Roy Williams
Snoo Wilson (two volumes)
David Wood (two volumes)
Victoria Wood

Methuen Film titles include

The Wings of the Dove
Hossein Armini

Mrs Brown
Jeremy Brock

Persuasion
Nick Dear after Jane Austen

The Gambler
Nick Dear after Dostoyevski

Beautiful Thing
Jonathan Harven

Little Voice
Mark Herman

The Long Good Friday
Barrie Keeffe

State and main
David Mamet

The Crucible
Arthur Miller

The English Patient
Anthony Minghella

The Talented Mr Ripley
Anthony Minghella

Twelfth Night
Trevor Nunn after Shakespeare

The Krays
Philip Ridley

The Reflecting Skin & The Passion of Darkly Noon
Philip Ridley

Trojan Eddie
Billy Roche

Sling Blade
Billy Bob Thornton

The Acid House
Irvine Welsh

Methuen World Classics

include

Jean Anouilh (two volumes)
Brendan Behan
Aphra Behn
Bertolt Brecht (eight volumes)
Büchner
Bulgakov
Calderón
Čapek
Anton Chekhov
Noël Coward (eight volumes)
Feydeau
Eduardo De Filippo
Max Frisch
John Galsworthy
Gogol
Gorky (two volumes)
Harley Granville Barker
 (two volumes)
Victor Hugo
Henrik Ibsen (six volumes)
Jarry

Lorca (three volumes)
Marivaux
Mustapha Matura
David Mercer (two volumes)
Arthur Miller (five volumes)
Molière
Musset
Peter Nichols (two volumes)
Joe Orton
A. W. Pinero
Luigi Pirandello
Terence Rattigan
 (two volumes)
W. Somerset Maugham
 (two volumes)
August Strindberg
 (three volumes)
J. M. Synge
Ramón del Valle-Inclán
Frank Wedekind
Oscar Wilde